PRESENTED TO

FROM

DATE

THE GOSPEL IN COLOR – FOR PARENTS

Text copyright © 2018 by Curtis A. Woods and Jarvis J. Williams
Illustration copyright © 2018 by Rommel Ruiz

All rights reserved. No part of this publication may be reproduced, distributed, or transmitted in any form or by any means, including photocopying, recording, or other electronic or mechanical methods, without the prior written permission of the publisher, except in the case of brief quotations embodied in critical reviews and certain other noncommercial uses permitted by copyright law.

First Edition 2018
Printed in China

ISBN-10: 0-9990835-7-0
ISBN-13: 978-0-9990835-7-4
ISBN-10: 1-7323099-0-6 (eBook)
ISBN-13: 978-1-7323099-0-6 (eBook)
Library of Congress Control Number: 2018943152

A **Patrol** Original Book

THE GOSPEL IN COLOR

EDITORIAL

CONTENT DIRECTOR
Eleazar Ruiz

WRITERS
Curtis A. Woods
Jarvis J. Williams

EDITOR
Pip Craighead

CREATIVE

ART DIRECTOR & ILLUSTRATOR
Rommel Ruiz

HEAD OF DESIGN
Eleazar Ruiz

ACKNOWLEDGMENTS

The idea for this book came as a result of a conversation that Jarvis had with Rommel and Eleazar Ruiz in Portland, Oregon, at the first Canvas Conference, sponsored by Humble Beast and Western Seminary. Jarvis' assignment at this conference was to talk about "The Idolatry of Race." After his talk, Rommel and Eleazar approached Jarvis regarding the possibility of a partnership in writing an illustrated book focusing on the gospel and racial reconciliation. After discussing a general direction and vision for the book in Portland and after ongoing conversations about the aim of the book, Jarvis, Rommel, and Eleazar agreed to proceed with the project. Realizing that the book would be much better if written with a brother with more knowledge of race issues, more experience teaching kids about race, and more experience in parenting, Jarvis asked his dear friend and big brother in the faith, Curtis, to partner with him to write this book. This book is the result of God's good providence to us.

There are many people to thank for helping this book become a reality. Many thanks to Humble Beast and Ryan Lister for inviting Jarvis to the first-ever Canvas Conference focusing on theology and the arts. Many thanks to Rommel and Eleazar for partnering with us in this work — especially for the illustrations. Many thanks to the entire team at Patrol for editorial advice and the nice reminders about our deadline.

Many thanks to Broadman & Holman Academic and The Witness: A Black Christian Collective for allowing Jarvis to use material in certain chapters that overlap with his book *One New Man: The Cross and Racial Reconciliation in Pauline Theology* (Nashville: B&H, 2010) and articles he wrote for The Witness website. We'd also be remiss if we failed to mention the many scholars who have awakened our consciousness to race matters — such as W. E. B. Du Bois *(The Souls of Black Folk)*, Alice Walker *(The Color Purple)*, Beverly Daniel Tatum

(Why Are All the Black Kids Sitting Together in the Cafeteria), David T. Wellman *(Portraits of White Racism)*, Joseph Barndt *(Dismantling Racism)*, Eduardo Bonilla-Silva *(Racism without Racists)*, Ibram X. Kendi *(Stamped From the Beginning)*, Cornel West ("Race and Modernity"), J. Kameron Carter *(Race: A Theological Account)*, Peggy McIntosh *(White Privilege: Unpacking The Invisible Knapsack)*, Michael O. Emerson and Christian Smith *(Divided by Faith)*, and Soong-Chan Rah *(The Next Evangelicalism)*. Their insights are evident in this book. Last, but certainly not least, we'd like to thank all the churches of the Kentucky Baptist Convention who are doing the hard work of fighting against racism in a racialized society, one conversation at a time. The heart of the matter is the matter of heart.

Finally, Curtis dedicates this book to Tracy, Anthony, Timothy, and Tristan Woods. Boys, your mom and I absolutely love bathing your minds in the gospel. The Father defines your worth, and union with the Son makes him delight in you by the Spirit. Jarvis dedicates this book to "Auntie" and "Uncle" Wendell who taught him much about love and justice.

Curtis A. Woods
Jarvis J. Williams
Louisville, Kentucky

CONTENTS

08   **Parents' Guide**
How to Use This Book

10   **Introduction**
Why This Book Now?

28   **Chapter 1**
What Is Race?

44   **Chapter 2**
What Is Racism?

68   **Chapter 3**
What Is the Good News of Jesus Christ?

86   **Chapter 4**
What Is Reconciliation?

102   **Conclusion**
The Gospel in Color

PARENTS' GUIDE
HOW TO USE THIS BOOK

This book is specifically designed so that you, as a parent, can dig deep into what the Bible says about race, racism, and reconciliation. To facilitate times of reflection and response, every chapter ends by giving you a specific framework for further study, thought, and prayer:

QUESTIONS TO CONSIDER Each chapter contains much food for thought, and these questions will help you reflect on your own life experiences, your view of the gospel, and how to respond to these pressing issues. Whether you consider these questions alone or with a reading companion, this section is designed to draw you into prayerful reflection and contemplation.

FURTHER READING Go deeper in exploring the issues covered in each chapter by reading a list of Scriptures covering the same topics, organized thematically.

At the end of each chapter, you'll also find the **Talking With Kids** section, which is designed to be used in conjunction with the companion book *The Gospel in Color — For Kids*. Since each chapter in this parents' book corresponds to the same chapter in the kids' book, you'll be able to help your child understood the themes covered in each reading, explaining concepts and vocab words while also helping your child complete the corresponding activity section of the companion book as needed. In each of these **Talking With Kids** sections, you'll find:

GOALS WHEN TEACHING YOUR CHILD Contains helpful objectives to keep in mind when talking with your child about the themes of each chapter.

WORDS TO EXPLAIN TO YOUR CHILD Contains succinct definitions of the vocab words covered in each chapter.

SCRIPTURE READING & REFLECTION WITH YOUR CHILD Contains specific Scriptures to read with your child along with themes to discuss afterward.

WAYS TO PRAY WITH YOUR CHILD Contains suggested prayer points to help you lead a time of prayer with your child based on the topics of each chapter.

Introduction

WHY THIS BOOK NOW?

By Jarvis J. Williams

WHY TEACH YOUR KIDS ABOUT THE GOSPEL AND RECONCILIATION?

I grew up in a rural town in the American South, in an environment where racism was part of the normal rhythm of everyday life, both in overt and covert forms. The ugly word "nigger" was a common white epithet for black people, one that black people internalized and used as well. As a black/brown person of mixed ethnic heritage, there were certain white communities I simply could not go to, and I still remember how certain individuals spoke of black people in dehumanizing ways, even to our faces. Growing up in that environment, I often struggled

> **"IS THERE SOMETHING WRONG WITH MY SKIN COLOR?"**

RACISM ISN'T JUST SOMETHING THAT HAPPENED IN THE PAST.

with the question: "Is there something wrong with my skin color?"

For almost two decades now, I've lived in a city and had the opportunity to preach and teach in diverse contexts throughout the country, and sadly, I've seen that racist ideologies and constructs exist beyond rural communities and small towns. The same ideas I grew up around are still present in highly populated, diverse, and well-educated cities — albeit in subtle and socially acceptable ways.

The book you hold in your hands exists because of this social reality. The fact is that we as parents need to talk with our children now about the underlying issues of racism and ethnic difference. Below are three pressing reasons why this is so vital.

REASON ONE: CURRENT RACIAL DIVISION

Racism isn't just something that happened in the past. One need only look at tragic events in the recent news to see that. Indeed, racism, ethnocentrism, and ethnic discrimination are deeply embedded within the American social fabric. Tragically, these evils have also entered into the church — despite racism's complete incompatibility with the gospel — and many Christians have stood on the wrong side of racial and ethnic justice in America. Consider, for example, the number of churches that fought against equal rights for blacks during slavery, reconstruction, and the era of Jim Crow laws. Consider also the way some people who identify as Christian speak to, about, or of brown immigrants particularly, as well as about black and brown people generally.

I remember the time my son overheard a child say he was stupid because he had "brown skin" — an event which occurred, sadly, within a predominantly white Christian context. I also recall a recent season in which my son was deeply grieved when he perceived expressions of racism in certain parts of American culture. One particular evening we spent a long time talking about the image of God, sin, racism, and the gospel, as he peppered me with tearful questions about these issues. Even as an eight-year-old, he recognized the way that the larger culture, and even Christian spaces, prioritized whiteness and marginalized his brown skin. As a Christian father, I must work diligently to assure my son that God loves his brown skin, that brown skin is beautiful, and that white skin is *not* superior to brown skin.

> **AS A CHRISTIAN FATHER, I MUST WORK DILIGENTLY TO ASSURE MY SON THAT GOD LOVES HIS BROWN SKIN AND THAT BROWN SKIN IS BEAUTIFUL.**

The reality of racial and ethnic division in our country today means that Christian parents of all ethnic backgrounds need to teach their kids about the gospel, race, racism, ethnic difference, and discrimination. Like it or not, as parents, we will be forced to have uncomfortable conversations with our children about these issues.

REASON TWO: COLOR-BLINDNESS ISN'T A SOLUTION

In response to racism, I've heard many well-meaning Christians and Christian parents espouse a naïve commitment to color-blindness. Essentially, color-blindness is the idea that we ought not to see color or make race-based decisions.

The concept of color-blindness at first seems appealing and even biblical. After all, we live in an age when many people of color have influence, power, and wealth — as evidenced by the fact that our country recently experienced a two-term black presidency. And *Galatians 3:28* states that "there is neither Jew nor Greek, neither slave nor free, and neither male nor female, for we are all one in Christ." As a result, some people argue that there is no such thing as a black Christian or a white Christian — we're all just Christians. People say that Christians should stop talking about race, because talking about race will make

> **COLOR-BLINDNESS INADVERTENTLY PERPETUATES THE VERY RACISM IT SEEKS TO AVOID.**

race an issue.

This color-blindness insists that ignoring race and looking beyond ethnic differences will lead us to a more racially equal and just society. Right? Wrong.

The problem with color-blindness is that Americans, including Christians, have inherited race-based social constructs based on a biological fiction (as we'll see in Chapter 2). As a result, our society continues to uphold structures and ideas which prioritize and marginalize groups based on their perceived race, in both intentional and unintentional ways. The truth of the matter is that so-called color-blindness will not create reconciled community, because racism and ethnic discrimination are deeply rooted in the American conscience and experience.

Regardless of how good color-blindness may sound to Christian parents, it's actually cruel and damaging to the many people who experience marginalization on a regular basis precisely because of their perceived race. Color-blindness inadvertently exacerbates the very racism it seeks to avoid, because it allows the majority cultural group to maintain their privileged position, continuing a social status quo in which minority groups continue to experience discrimination and domination. Christian parents who affirm color-blindness do a great racial injustice to their kids and to the black and brown people in their churches and communities, deepening racial wounds and setting up children for emotional, spiritual, and psychological devastation when they do experience racism.

> **WE ALL LIVE IN A RACIALIZED SOCIETY, WHERE ONE'S PERCEIVED RACE PROVIDES ADVANTAGES OR DISADVANTAGES IN SOCIAL INTERACTIONS AND ACHIEVEMENTS.**

So no matter how hard we try to deny these facts and look beyond the color of one's skin, we live in a country which makes decisions based on false beliefs about skin color and race. Ethnic discrimination is part of the ordinary and everyday rhythm of the American experience — and so we must address it frankly and wisely, by the power of the Spirit.

REASON THREE: RACISM IS A SYSTEMIC PROBLEM

As the following chapters will demonstrate, my co-author Curtis and I believe that racism and ethnic discrimination possess both individual and systemic dimensions. We also believe that these forms of discrimination are deeply ingrained in the structural fabric of the United States, including within many Christian spaces and institutions, often showing up in subtle ways.

We are not saying that every individual person intentionally practices racist behavior against those from a different race, nor does this necessarily mean every problem experienced by black and brown people in America or in any given context results from racism.

But like it or not, we all live in a racialized society, where one's perceived race provides advantages or disadvantages in social interactions and achievements. And many of the challenges black and brown people have historically experienced in the U.S. (such as slavery, Jim Crow, and the exploitation of immigrant workers) have been directly caused by racism. In the American experience, racial injustice has been especially evident between blacks and whites, but can also be seen amongst other marginalized groups as well. Native Americans, Asians, Latinos, the Irish, Jews, Arabs, and many other groups have experienced racism and discrimination simply because of their perceived differences.

American history, tragically, is marred by the legacy of a social order which placed non-white men, women, and children — people created in the image of God — at the bottom, and the destructive effects of this social order are arguably still felt today.

AN INVITATION

The reality of racism is a deeply important issue for parents to grapple with, especially because it is ultimately a spiritual problem. As we shall see in the following chapters, racism's origins go all the way back to the Garden of Eden, and the sin of racism can only find complete healing through the victory of Jesus Christ on the cross. That's why this book seeks to equip parents to have honest, fruitful conversations with their children about the issues of race, ethnic divisions, and racial reconciliation in a way which is gospel-centered and biblically accurate.

My co-author Curtis and I are two African-American men from different backgrounds, with diverse cultural and educational experiences. In the following chapters, we'll discuss what the Bible says about race, where the modern idea of race originated, where racism comes from, and how the good news of Jesus brings about healing and unity in the area of ethnic difference. Throughout this book, you'll find biblical exposition, concise definitions of key terms, real-life examples, and personal stories, along with visual illustrations to help illuminate the content.
We know it's not necessarily easy to talk about these things with your kids, so we designed the book to work hand in

RACISM'S ORIGINS GO ALL THE WAY BACK TO THE GARDEN OF EDEN, AND THE SIN OF RACISM CAN ONLY FIND COMPLETE HEALING THROUGH THE VICTORY OF JESUS CHRIST ON THE CROSS.

hand with a companion book written specifically for children: *The Gospel in Color — For Kids*. After reading through each chapter of this *Parents* book, you can read through the *Kids* version with your children, explaining vocabulary words, reading Scripture, and praying together. The content in this book will help you walk through conversations with your kids in order to help equip them to view the world through a robust gospel lens.

Before we begin, we'd like to briefly note that portions of this book speak honestly about the historical and ongoing reality of racism and its effects, many of which were perpetrated by people of European descent. While we seek to accurately reflect this truth, we would never want our white brothers and sisters to read this book under the weight of condemnation. Our goal is to speak the truth in love, and this book is intended to be something that everyone can read and learn from. Our hope is that any readers who realize they have held racist attitudes would lament and repent as the Spirit convicts their hearts; other readers may become aware for the first time of the privileges they enjoy in American society because of their white skin color. In any case, the truth of the matter is that we are all sinners, and we all need God's grace and forgiveness, which is readily available to us in Christ.

Our prayer is that the Spirit would use our work to help you teach your kids the message of gospel-centered racial reconciliation. May this book support you as you lead your kids in seeking the unification of all things and people in Christ through the gospel. Our hope is that our book would celebrate the beauty of the gospel in color, and that together as believers, we would proclaim our unity within our diversity, and teach our kids to do the same.

> **MAY THIS BOOK SUPPORT YOU AS YOU LEAD YOUR KIDS IN SEEKING THE UNIFICATION OF ALL THINGS AND PEOPLE IN CHRIST THROUGH THE GOSPEL.**

"SO GOD CREATED MAN IN HIS OWN IMAGE,
IN THE IMAGE OF GOD HE CREATED HIM;
MALE AND FEMALE HE CREATED THEM."

–Genesis 1:27 (ESV)

Chapter One

WHAT IS RACE?

By Curtis A. Woods

BIG IDEA

To understand the truth about race, we need to turn to the Bible. There we see that God made all people in the image of God. As image-bearers, human beings were made to reflect who God is, to wisely care for God's creation, and to treat each other with dignity and respect. Biblical truth reveals there is only one race… the human race. Yet in stark contrast to this, the modern concept of race arose within the last few centuries, as key thinkers in the European Enlightenment claimed that human beings could be divided up into different racial categories of varying value. They taught that some races were superior to others, and as a result, this lie was used to justify centuries of oppression and cruelty.

IMPORTANT QUESTIONS

I responded to the gospel in 1994. The Holy Spirit showed me my sins, and I realized that I was a merciless person who needed the Lord's mercy. After deciding to follow Jesus as Lord and Savior, God gave me a love for Scripture. I started reading the book of *Genesis* — and I discovered a whole new way of looking at the world.

Now, many years later, as a Christian parent who affirms the authority of Scripture, I often ask myself: Why is there so much confusion concerning the meaning of race? When we speak about certain skin colors as indicators of fixed racial categories, do such statements fit the narrative of Scripture? Or is our understanding of race informed by a worldly intellectual system created just a few centuries ago — one which represents a demonic attack on the goodness of God's creation?

Just as I first read the Bible as a Christian to make sense of the world, so too, we need to look to the Bible to truly understand race — so that we see God's creation through God-centered eyes.

BACK TO THE BEGINNING

The opening chapters of *Genesis* show us how God created the world out of nothing by speaking all things into existence. He created the heavens and the earth, the seas and the dry land. He filled the earth with vegetation, made the sun and moon, and populated the world with living creatures on sea and land and air. All these creatures were fruitful and multiplied their species on the earth and in the sea. God was happy with what he had made *(Genesis 1:20-25)*.

Lastly, God created the crowning jewel of creation — Adam and Eve — in his image, giving them the task of acting as stewards over his world. No other creature could help them fulfill God's command. God was deeply pleased with his creation and rested to enjoy his artistry *(Genesis 1:26-2:3)*.

The creation account presents a beautiful picture of love. God cared for his creation by crafting a world that could sustain the physical and emotional needs of humanity. The man and woman loved and trusted one another without fear *(Genesis 2:23-25)*. The animals and sea creatures enjoyed their habitats without territorial fighting. It was literally *all good!*

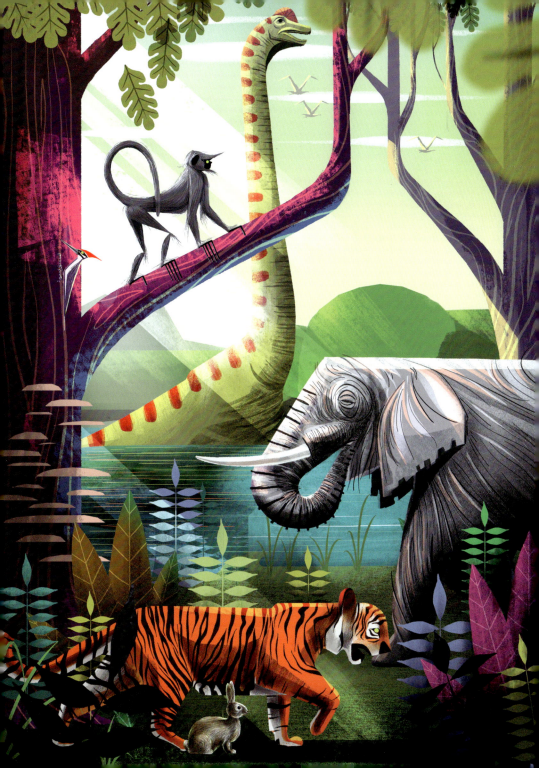

THE TRUTH ABOUT RACE

As we see in the *Genesis* account, God created every family from the loving relationship of the first man and woman. Thus, according to Scripture, every human being has a common ancestor *(Acts 17:26)*. It's extremely important to understand that when the Bible utilizes words referring to race and ethnic difference, it is not referring to the modern conception of racial categories of differing value. The Bible clearly rejects the idea of a special race of people who sit above other skin colors.

EVERY COLOR WAS MADE TO BE LOVED AND CHERISHED, BECAUSE GOD CREATED ALL THINGS GOOD.

The Bible is clear that there are not different races of human beings in the sense of different categories of people. Every person is made in God's image, and as such, has a unique worth and identity.

Each skin color on the earth points back to the first person created from the earth — Adam *(Genesis 2:7)*. God's vision was for all colors to love one another and treat one another with dignity. To label different hues as inferior goes against the clear teaching of Scripture.

THE LIE ABOUT RACE

The modern conception of race is a fictional construct developed to separate humans based on color. In contrast to God's word, which depicts the commonality of all people, the idea of race was created to uplift one skin color as superior to other colors and ethnicities.

During the European Enlightenment in the 18th century, influential intellectual figures like Immanuel Kant invented racial categories which privileged Europeans as inherently superior to other ethnicities. They taught that there were multiple, radically different races rather than one human race. Respected thinkers in a variety of academic disciplines advanced theories to support their preconceived notions of white superiority.

As this imaginary concept of race caricatured and oppressed any ethnic group branded inferior, many Europeans learned to see non-European individuals as inferior beings — even though the same color of blood runs through all our veins. Since "lesser colors" were viewed as less than human, they could be bought and sold like property, justifying slavery.

Some of these European false teachers were religious, so they dishonorably used the Bible as a source to explain God's greater love for white people over other shades in the global community. Claiming that non-white Europeans lacked a special connection to God, white Europeans thought they had a manifest destiny to determine the potential value and economic use of non-whites.

In so doing, these thinkers rejected the biblical teaching that all people, in every shade of skin, are precious in the sight of the Lord; instead, they exchanged truth for the lie of racial superiority. Essentially, they developed a fictional creation story – a twisted alternative to the biblical account. They used their imaginations against God himself, seeking to create a new story of the world.

Yet the biblical testimony has always testified clearly to the equality of human beings, and the power of the gospel breaks down the lies of racial superiority. God wants to give us new eyes to see all the colors of humanity without fear or anger. Every color was made to be loved and cherished, because God created all things good. We are each a part of God's good creation,

WHEN YOU SEE THE GOSPEL IN COLOR, THE WORLD BECOMES BEAUTIFUL AGAIN.

and all human colors are valuable because they bear God's image. When you see the gospel in color, the world becomes beautiful again.

So where does the destructive lie of racism actually come from? What is its ultimate root? The very *Genesis* account we just considered contains the answer, as we'll see in the next chapter.

QUESTIONS TO CONSIDER

1. Are you shocked to learn that the modern conception of race is a fictional construct? How does the concept of separate racial categories shape relationships in Western culture?
2. What kind of understanding of race did you grow up with?
3. How have you seen people believe the lie of racism, whether in overt or subtle ways? How can you be part of the solution and share the biblical truth to counter this lie?
4. Are there any ways you have absorbed the lie of racism, or felt a temptation to view your ethnic heritage as superior or inferior to that of other ethnicities?

FURTHER READING

- God made humanity's first parents, Adam and Eve, in his image: *Genesis 1-2*
- God made all humanity with dignity and honor: *Genesis 1:27; Psalm 8; Psalm 139*
- God calls all people into his kingdom, from every people group on earth: *Revelation 5:9-10, 7:9-10*

TALKING WITH KIDS

GOALS WHEN TEACHING YOUR CHILD

1. Help your child understand that God made the world and everything in it, and that he saw his creation as good.

2. Help your child understand that the Bible does not teach that people belong to separate racial categories of differing value. Instead, the Bible teaches that all people are made in the image of God, which means they have great worth.

3. Help your child understand that the idea that some skin colors and ethnicities are better than others is a lie, and that the Bible teaches that all skin colors are of equal value.

WORDS TO EXPLAIN TO YOUR CHILD

Equal: Having the same worth and value.

Race: A word which can simply refer to the human race or a specific ethnic group, but which can be falsely used to mean a category of people with an inherently different value than other people.

SCRIPTURE READING & REFLECTION WITH YOUR CHILD

Read the creation account in *Genesis 1-2*. Discuss what it means that all people are descended from the first man and woman, Adam and Eve, and that all people are made in the image of God.

WAYS TO PRAY WITH YOUR CHILD

- Give God thanks for the fact that he made the world and all things in it, and praise him that you and your child have the incredible honor of being made in the image of God.
- Pray that God would help people of all skin colors see that he is the one who made them, and that he made us all to bear his image and treat one another with love and respect.
- Give God praise that the way he made you and your child — including your skin color and ethnic heritage — is no mistake, and that your skin color and ethnic heritage are good.
- Pray that God would give you eyes to see his hand in the wonderful diversity of all people in the world, and thank him that he is the God of every tribe, tongue, people, and nation.

"YOU SHALL TREAT THE STRANGER WHO SOJOURNS WITH YOU AS THE NATIVE AMONG YOU, AND YOU SHALL LOVE HIM AS YOURSELF, FOR YOU WERE STRANGERS IN THE LAND OF EGYPT: I AM THE LORD YOUR GOD."

–Leviticus 19:34 (ESV)

Chapter Two

WHAT IS RACISM?

By Curtis A. Woods

BIG IDEA

Where does racial conflict come from? To find the answer, we turn once more to the Bible, where we see the origin of human sin. Adam and Eve's rebellious disobedience in the Garden of Eden has led to all the conflict and pain we see in our world today — including the sin of racism. Racism is a sinful proclivity that deems another image-bearer a problem based on skin color or ethnic difference. Within American history, racism has led to systemic oppression, chattel slavery, and an ongoing social system of race-based privileges and disadvantages.

A REMARK AT PLAYTIME

The first time my eldest son encountered racism was at a predominantly Anglo-American Baptist church located in a small Kentucky city. He was six years old. As the only person of color in his Sunday school class, he knew that his skin tone was different than the other children, but he never assumed it was a problem. But one day, during playtime, an Anglo child made an insensitive remark, planting a seed in my son's imagination that said he was not special because he was not white. My son was confused and crushed. One evening he asked my wife and me, "How can I change my color?"

> **NOT ONLY DO THE OPENING CHAPTERS OF GENESIS SHOW US WHERE HUMANITY COMES FROM, WE DISCOVER THE ORIGIN OF RACISM AS WELL.**

Initially, his question and tears touched a nerve deep within my heart. I was ready to have strong words with the child's parents. But instead of immediately confronting them, my wife and I comforted our son through prayer and Scripture meditation. We wanted to make sure that the lie in my son's mind would be rebuked and uprooted before it germinated and did catastrophic damage to his view of the world and himself.

Then, after speaking with our pastors, we confronted the situation with compassion and conviction. As Christian parents, we could not sit idly by while racism's evil seed festered in the minds of these two boys. Both the victimizer and victim needed counsel. One child's belief required correction while the other child's emotions needed protection. When encountering a situation like this, it is natural to wonder: where does the lie of racism come from?

THE ORIGIN OF SIN

Not only do the opening chapters of *Genesis* show us where humanity comes from, we discover the origin of racism as well. *Genesis 3* tells us how evil stole its way into God's good creation through a lying serpent. The serpent told Adam and Eve that God could not be trusted, insinuating that God wanted to withhold something good from the first family. He convinced Eve that God was jealous and insecure. As Eve listened to this voice questioning God's sovereignty and goodness, she decided to separate from God's authority and disobey God's command. In a sense, she wanted to be her own god by changing God's instruction to fit her own desires. This is the very essence of sin.

Eve and Adam both defied God's command not to eat from the Tree of the Knowledge of Good and Evil, thus bringing the destruction of sin into the beauty of Eden. As a result, death came into the world, and humanity's innocence was ended. Adam and Eve's relationship with God and with one another was shattered and twisted.

After the fall of mankind, there was global strife on earth. Men and women had fights with one another, and groups of people divided based on their differences, even though all people bear God's image. Farming became burdensome. Animals attacked humans and ate other animals. God had created an orderly cosmos, but sin birthed chaos.

THE SIN OF RACISM

Since the fall, the serpent continues to spread lies about God's original good creation. The lie of race which we considered in the last chapter is the fruit of this same poisoned seed. This lie leads to racism, a sinful proclivity that deems another image-bearer a problem based on skin color or ethnic difference.

Racism within a society leads to laws and social norms designed to keep ethnic minorities "in their place" while advancing the status of those in the ethnic majority. As a result, individuals are labeled problems simply because of their ethnic background. You can be declared a criminal or potential threat based on your ethnicity, rather than your actions. These false labels create a system of advantage for the "superior race" while creating a disadvantage for others — even though everyone is an image-bearer of God.

> **A COUNTRY THAT CLAIMED "IN GOD WE TRUST" ENACTED LAWS WHICH SEPARATED FAMILIES AND DEPRIVED MOTHERS AND FATHERS OF PARENTAL AUTHORITY OVER THEIR CHILDREN...**

AMERICAN SLAVERY

Within American history, the legacy of slavery is one of the most tangible manifestations of racism's effects. For centuries, human beings were treated as property — "chattel" — and forcibly taken from their homes in Africa, placed in warehouses, and transported all over the globe like cargo in the bottom of rat-infested ships. Children were kidnapped from their mothers and fathers. Many people died during these voyages to slave ports.

In chains, enslaved families were separated and sold on auction blocks to keep their captors out of debt. They were given to the highest bidder to live a life of slavery, a life in which they had no human rights. Their masters could do anything they desired to them, even treating them like disposable items. Each enslaved African was deprived of their God-given human dignity — an act which ultimately dishonors God.

SLAVERY MAY HAVE BEEN OVER, BUT THE COUNTRY CONTINUED TO GRANT PRIVILEGES TO A WHITE MAJORITY WHILE OPPRESSING PEOPLE OF COLOR AND OTHER MINORITY GROUPS.

It is ironic that despite the supposed freedom that America stood for, the state-sanctioned institution of slavery blocked people from experiencing life, liberty, and the pursuit of happiness. Not only were kidnapped black and brown individuals enslaved, but American laws supported hereditary slavery — meaning any child born to an enslaved black mother, even if his or her father was a free black or white man, was automatically the owner's lifetime property. A country that claimed "In God We Trust" enacted laws which separated families and deprived mothers and fathers of parental authority over their children, even as these oppressed people gave blood, sweat, and tears to build the nation.

America's founding documents themselves reflect the deep influence of racism during the country's inception. The Declaration of Independence called for universal liberty based on natural rights given by the Creator — but the constitutional framers removed specific antislavery language from the Declaration to appease slaveholding delegates. Many framers of the Constitution held sympathies toward the gradual emancipation of enslaved Africans, even while they rejected the biblical belief that every human being has equal worth and dignity before God.

SYSTEMIC OPPRESSION

Frederick Douglass, a 19th-century Christian abolitionist and intellectual who challenged institutional racism, wrote about the crippling social consequences of slavery: "We are then a persecuted people; not because we are colored, but simply because that color has for a series of years been coupled in the public mind with the degradation of slavery and servitude." In other words, black and brown people were stigmatized as unequal by a society that privileged whiteness.

True to Douglass' words, racial oppression continued even after the Civil War's conclusion. Though the Emancipation Proclamation officially ended slavery in Confederate states and parishes, Jim Crow laws were established throughout the United States under Rutherford B. Hayes to ensure that whites retained the upper hand in American society. State-sanctioned segregation and oppression continued for a century of American history. Slavery may have been over, but the country continued to grant privileges to a white majority while oppressing people of color and other minority groups. Whiteness, as an idea of universal purity, defined rightness in every sphere of political engagement. This dangerous idea poisoned potential friendships between white, black, and brown people for many years to come.

Beyond slavery and Jim Crow laws, individuals from a wide variety of ethnic backgrounds have experienced oppression through centuries of American history, whether through explicit legislation such as the Chinese Exclusion Act and the Indian Removal Act, or hurtful cultural caricatures and subtle social oppression. Many people groups have been marginalized and discriminated against in the past (as well as in the present), including Asians, Jews, Iranians, Arabs, Native Americans, Latinos, Italians, Romanis, and others, simply because of their perceived difference or immigrant status.

Today, the legacy of slavery and racism sadly continues. The fact that for centuries, America's laws officially privileged whiteness means that children of color are still affected by these structural systems of advantage, even when explicitly racist laws have been ended. Many individuals in minority populations have worked hard to achieve

CHRISTIANS ARE CALLED TO HONOR GOD BY SPEAKING THE TRUTH AGAINST RACISM IN A GRACIOUS WAY, WHILE SEEKING TO UNDO RACISM'S DEVASTATING EFFECTS.

equitable employment opportunities by exemplifying character, competence, and commitment in the workplace, yet they have discovered that a glass ceiling prevents them from achieving the highest positions in predominantly white spaces.

This history of lopsided privilege has fostered an atmosphere of social animosity and racial tension. Those who are perpetually unprivileged often refuse to build up a society that limits advancement opportunities. Meanwhile, many white people have not realized or acknowledged that they have received benefits from a history of racial privilege — and, worse still, some have shown a lack of genuine concern for the cries of injustice from the unprivileged. Racial privilege sickens the foundational soul of a nation.

WHERE DO WE GO FROM HERE?

As Christians, we are not called to despair over the reality of racism nor to hate those who hold to racist ideas. Instead, Christians are called to honor God by speaking the truth against racism in a gracious way, while seeking to undo racism's devastating effects. That means we should not see people who have racist ideas as the enemy. They are victims of mankind's oldest enemy, Satan, who is the true author of racist ideas. He hates God's beautiful creation, and spreads lies to destroy it.

If you encounter a person who hates people because of their skin color or perceived ethnic difference, you are hearing the serpent's voice.

The good news is that even after sin first entered the world, God promised to restore humanity's vertical and horizontal relationships alike *(Genesis 3:15)*. He vowed to redeem the impact that Adam's sin had brought upon the entire world. God's promise of restoration includes the reconciliation of diverse groups of people to God and to one another, as we'll see in the next chapter.

QUESTIONS TO CONSIDER

1. How is racism similar to that first sin in the Garden?
2. How should the spiritual nature of racism affect the way we speak about ethnic divisions?
3. How does the gospel give us the resources to counter the lie of racism?
4. Jesus calls us to do good to our enemies and pray for those who persecute us. How can we recognize the evil of racism without hating those who propagate this lie?

FURTHER READING

- Sin shattered humanity's relationship with God and with one another: *Genesis 3; Romans 5; Romans 6:23*
- Racism is a sin: *James 2:8-9; 1 John 2:11; Leviticus 19:33-34; 1 John 4:19-21*
- God promised he would defeat the seed of the serpent by means of the seed of the woman: *Genesis 3:15*

TALKING WITH KIDS

GOALS WHEN TEACHING YOUR CHILD

- Help your child understand that sin is an act of rebellion against God and an attack on the goodness of God's world.
- Help your child see that racism is a sinful lie, one which goes against the truth that God made all people in his image.
- Help your child understand that the idea that some people are better than others is a lie which many people have taught over the years. Even though this lie still affects our world today, the good news of Jesus is stronger than any lie.

WORDS TO EXPLAIN TO YOUR CHILD

- **Sin:** An act of rebellion against God and his good laws.
- **Racism:** The poisonous idea of people or governments rewarding social and economic privileges to one group of people by virtue of skin color or ethnic background.

SCRIPTURE READING & REFLECTION WITH YOUR CHILD

Read the account of the fall in *Genesis 3*. Discuss what sin is (rebellion against God) and why it is so serious. Talk about the fact that all the pain, evil, and sadness we see in the world comes from sin, and that Jesus came into the world to forgive our sins and overcome the consequence of sin, which is death.

WAYS TO PRAY WITH YOUR CHILD

- Ask your child if he or she has ever been cruel to someone because they were different, whether they had a different skin color or simply acted differently. If so, pray with your child to ask God for forgiveness for that sin, and ask him to give your child wisdom in how to apologize to that person, if at all possible.

- Is there anybody your child has a hard time showing kindness to because they are different than them? Ask God to help you and your child to see that person the way he would have you see them — as someone loved by God.

- Ask your child if he or she has heard anybody say something racist. If so, pray for that person, and ask God for wisdom on any ways your child can lovingly, graciously correct those words (as appropriate to the situation). Ask God to heal any pain those racist words have caused your child.

"BEHOLD, THE LAMB OF GOD,
WHO TAKES AWAY THE SIN OF THE WORLD!"
–John 1:29 (ESV)

Chapter Three

WHAT IS THE GOOD NEWS OF JESUS CHRIST?

By Jarvis J. Williams

BIG IDEA

The overarching narrative of the Bible shows us how God's good creation was marred by the entrance of sin, which lies at the root of all forms of racial and ethnic division. Yet after the fall, God promised that he would send a Savior — a prophecy fulfilled by Jesus Christ, God become man. The good news of Jesus' life, death, and resurrection is the best news possible for our world, and as Christians are shaped by the gospel, ethnic and racial divisions are healed.

A MESSAGE OF GREAT JOY

As a parent, it's always a delight to see a child excited about good news. My wife and I love it when our son is excited to share something with us. And there's no greater delight as a parent than to see your child get excited about the gospel. I recall a specific occasion when I walked into our nine-year-old son's room while he was praying, and after he finished, he gave me a big bear hug. He exclaimed: "Daddy, I'm so happy!" and I asked why. He responded with a smile: "Because I repented of my sins and asked Jesus to make me his faithful servant." As his father, I thought: this is good news indeed.

> **GOD'S PROMISE OF RESTORATION INCLUDES THE RECONCILIATION OF DIVERSE GROUPS OF PEOPLE TO GOD AND TO ONE ANOTHER...**

A LONG-AWAITED ANNOUNCEMENT

In fact, the gospel of Jesus Christ isn't just really, really good news; it's actually the best news of all! The actual word *gospel* refers to an announcement — specifically, the announcement that God has fulfilled all of his saving promises for all people, regardless of ethnic or racial distinction, redeeming a fallen creation through Jesus Christ.

To put this good news in context, we need to understand the overarching narrative of the Bible. As we saw in the opening chapters of *Genesis*, God's original creation was beautiful and in perfect harmony. The climax of his creation was humanity. However, when the serpent entered the Garden of Eden, he deceived the woman, and she deceived the man. Sin opened their innocent eyes. In righteous response, God cursed the entire creation with judgment. Sin shattered the man and woman's relationship with God and with one another; sin brought the curse of death into the world. Yet God promised that he would defeat the seed of the serpent by means of the seed of the woman *(Genesis 3:15)*.

Adam and Eve fled from God when they sinned, and their son Cain murdered his brother, Abel, because of sin *(Genesis 4:1-8)*. But God promised to restore humanity's vertical and horizontal relationships alike. He also promised to redeem the impact that Adam's sin had brought upon the entire world. God's promise of restoration includes the reconciliation of diverse groups of people to God and to one another, as well as the restoration of the entire universe.

> **SIMPLY PUT, WITHOUT JESUS, THERE IS NO GOOD NEWS, INCLUDING IN THE AREA OF RACIAL RECONCILIATION.**

THE GOOD NEWS AND ITS RESULT

In the New Testament, the cross and resurrection of Jesus Christ are the foundation of the gospel of Jesus Christ *(1 Corinthians 15:3-8)*. Jesus' death and resurrection guarantee that God has accomplished reconciliation for all in Christ and that he has fulfilled his promise to renew and restore everything lost in the Garden of Eden because of sin's curse *(Genesis 3:15)*. The good news that diverse groups of people can repent of their sin, enter into the kingdom of God, confess Jesus as Lord, call upon the name of the Lord, and be saved from God's judgment can only be a true announcement if Jesus died and resurrected in bodily form. Simply put, without Jesus, there is no good news, including in the area of racial reconciliation.

God's work of salvation through the cross and resurrection of Jesus Christ is seen on a personal level when enemies become reconciled friends in Christ. We see this most clearly when the apostle Paul became a Christian. Paul was initially a violent persecutor of the church, but after placing faith in Christ, Paul lived as an incredible ambassador of reconciliation. Paul's ministry shows us that God's act of reconciling the world to himself through Christ is the foundation for God's reconciliation of diverse people to himself and to one another in Christ *(Ephesians 2:11-3:8)*.

Soon after Paul became a Christian, he toiled to unify all things and all people in Christ through the gospel without ethnic distinction. He helped people understand that in Jesus, ethnic identities are transformed, but not erased. God used him to not only spread the gospel, but to urge people from diverse backgrounds to live in reconciled community with each other *(Galatians 3:28)*.

Paul taught that neither Jews nor Gentiles should require one another to forfeit the distinct and beautiful aspects of their ethnic identities which were in step with the gospel and the Spirit. All people are justified by faith in Christ apart from the works of the law and are transformed by the power of the Spirit. Each distinct ethnic group in Christ is made to experience new creation, while still maintaining aspects of their distinct ethnic identities *(Galatians 2:16-5:26)*.

THE RENEWAL OF ALL THINGS

Just as the fall of Adam and Eve in the Garden brought a universal curse upon the entire world, Jesus' cross and resurrection renew and transform the entire fallen universe. The Spirit enables different ethnicities, skin colors, genders, and classes of people to live in pursuit of reconciled unity with one another in Christ through the gospel. One way this renewal is visibly expressed

EACH DISTINCT ETHNIC GROUP IN CHRIST IS MADE TO EXPERIENCE NEW CREATION, WHILE STILL MAINTAINING ASPECTS OF THEIR DISTINCT ETHNIC IDENTITIES.

in the world is when Spirit-empowered, racially and ethnically diverse believers begin to live in reconciled community with each other as they sit under the apostles' teaching, share resources with each other, spend time in one another's homes, bear each other's burdens, and praise the Lord together with glad hearts *(Acts 2:42-47)*.

The gospel of Jesus Christ is the announcement that God will restore this fallen universe in and through the death and resurrection of Jesus Christ *(Revelation 5:9-10)*. His diverse, redeemed people will reign on a transformed and glorified earth forever in perfect reconciled community with their Jewish King Jesus, while continuing to maintain their different beautiful skin colors.

In short, the dark-skinned Jesus died to redeem many colors. This gospel is truly good news! It's the best news for diverse ethnicities and races of people alienated from God and from each other because of sin and because of the racism, ethnocentrism, and discrimination which sin has produced. The good news of Jesus Christ announces that God has acted in Christ Jesus to deal with the power of sin over the entire creation.

QUESTIONS TO CONSIDER

1. How should the gospel shape the way you view racial reconciliation?
2. How did Jesus' atoning sacrifice for sin and victorious resurrection bring together people from different backgrounds in the first-century church?
3. What does it mean that in Jesus, ethnic identities are transformed, but not erased?
4. How does the good news of Jesus provide the strongest possible foundation for racial reconciliation?

FURTHER READING

- Jesus' death and resurrection guarantee that God has accomplished reconciliation for all in Christ, fulfilling his promise to renew and restore everything lost in the Garden of Eden because of sin's curse: *Genesis 3:15; Isaiah 65:17-25; Romans 5:12-21, 8:18-39; Galatians 1:3-4, 6:15; Revelation 21-22*

- Jesus' resurrection is our only hope of restoration: *1 Corinthians 15:12-19; Ephesians 2:11-3:8*

- Jesus died and rose from the dead to draw all people to

himself: *John 1:29, 3:16, 12:32; Romans 3:21-5:11; 1 Corinthians 15; Ephesians 1:7-10; 1 John 2:2, 4:7-21*

TALKING WITH KIDS

GOALS WHEN TEACHING YOUR CHILD

- Help your child comprehend where sin started (in the Garden of Eden, as we saw in Chapter 2) and understand that sin is radically destructive, both in terms of our relationship with God and our relationship with other people.

- Help your child realize that the only cure for sin and hope for restoration is found in Jesus' life, death, and resurrection — a cure he gives us freely out of his great love for each and every one of us.

- Help your child understand that the good news of Jesus affects the way we live our lives now — and brings healing not just between us and God, but between ourselves and people from different racial and ethnic backgrounds.

WORDS TO EXPLAIN TO YOUR CHILD

- **Resurrection:** The act of someone being raised from death to life. Jesus was resurrected after his death on the cross, and because of Jesus, all who believe in his name have the future promise of being raised from death to everlasting life.
- **Gospel:** The good news that through Jesus' life, death, resurrection, and ascension (going into heaven to rule our world with his Father), the kingdom of God has come and all can be saved through faith in him.

SCRIPTURE READING & REFLECTION WITH YOUR CHILD

Read *1 Corinthians 15:20-23* and talk about why the good news of Jesus' life, death, and resurrection is the greatest reason for rejoicing that we could ever have.

WAYS TO PRAY WITH YOUR CHILD

- Thank God for the forgiveness and redemption we have in Jesus' freely given sacrifice. Rejoice in the fact that the Lord counts you and your child as his beloved children because you've put your faith in him.

- Pray that everyone in your family would continually turn to Jesus for forgiveness and restoration whenever they sin, knowing that Christ has already paid the price for sinners — including if they sin by regarding one skin color as better than another.

- Pray that people all over the world who do not know Jesus would come to experience forgiveness and peace with God through the gospel. Pray that this good news would bring healing to all those who are divided over skin color and other issues.

- Is there anyone your child knows who they'd like to share the good news of Jesus with? Ask God how your child can tell them about Jesus, and pray for an opportunity to share this exciting news with them. Give your child advice on how to share the gospel.

"ALL THIS IS FROM GOD, WHO THROUGH CHRIST RECONCILED US TO HIMSELF AND GAVE US THE MINISTRY OF RECONCILIATION…"

–2 Corinthians 5:18 (ESV)

Chapter Four

WHAT IS RECONCILIATION?

By Jarvis J. Williams

BIG IDEA

Reconciliation is part of the very heart of the gospel, and the good news of Jesus includes the mending of broken relationships between different ethnic groups. As Christians, we are called to be a community made up of reconciled people who are marked by love for one another and whose racial divisions are healed and redeemed.

A STORY OF RECONCILIATION

One of the most powerful stories of reconciliation in the Bible is the story of the prodigal son. In *Luke 15:11-32*, Jesus shared this powerful tale of a father who had two sons. The older son seemed to serve his father well, while the younger son did not serve his father well. The younger son asked for his inheritance, then left his family and wasted all of his money on parties, food, and friends.

After wasting his money, the younger son ran back home to beg his father's forgiveness. As the father saw his son coming from a distance, he rushed to meet him. He embraced him and kissed him, and then celebrated his younger son's return with a party. The older son who had stayed home and served his father complained that his father had showed the younger son too much affection. The father exclaimed to the older son that the son who returned was lost, but now was found. His return home was a reason to celebrate!

The father's response to his younger son is a beautiful picture of reconciliation. The younger son acted as an enemy when he abandoned his father. But when he returned to his father after coming to his senses, the father received him as a friend.

This is the heart of reconciliation: when enemies become friends. We use the phrase *racial reconciliation* to refer to the restoration of broken relationships between diverse ethnic groups and skin colors within the human race.

RECONCILIATION IS NOT OPTIONAL

Reconciliation is part of the Christian gospel. Jesus' death and resurrection reconcile image-bearers to God and to one another. This is the mystery of the gospel *(Ephesians 1:9-3:13)*. Ethnically diverse groups of people have equal access to God and the Spirit by faith in Jesus Christ and are co-heirs of his promises of salvation through the gospel, because Christ died for their sins and was resurrected from the dead to draw all men to himself.

> **THIS IS THE HEART OF RECONCILIATION: WHEN ENEMIES BECOME FRIENDS.**

As Curtis discussed in the previous chapters, both racism and the very concept of race in the American experience are tremendous sources of social and spiritual alienation. Race in our context is uniquely connected to fictional racial categories, white supremacy, and the history of racism in our country. But even though the understanding of race and racial division is different in other parts of the world, the need for racial reconciliation is universal and global — and vitally important.

The gospel explicitly addresses the issue of ethnic difference, and the reconciliation and unity of all things and all people in Christ *(Ephesians 2:11-22)*.

In fact, ethnic division was an issue present during the early church, in which Jews and Gentiles — two groups from radically different backgrounds — were united by their common faith in Jesus. When divisions and tension arose, the apostle Paul commanded both parties to receive one another, not to judge one another, and to bear each other's weaknesses *(Romans 14)*. Paul's command is just as relevant to us now; we must actively, passionately seek racial reconciliation today, in our context.

Jesus' death for sin included a death for the sin of racism. Racism makes people enemies of one another, but Jesus' death and resurrection can reconcile enemies and make them friends — and not merely friends, but brothers and sisters in Christ. This reconciliation of groups of people previously divided by racism is a powerful example of how the gospel of Jesus Christ accomplishes friendship and unity where there was once enmity.

> **THE GOSPEL EXPLICITLY ADDRESSES THE ISSUE OF ETHNIC DIFFERENCE, AND THE RECONCILIATION AND UNITY OF ALL THINGS AND ALL PEOPLE IN CHRIST.**

A PEOPLE MARKED BY UNITY

Jesus prayed for his followers to experience this kind of gospel unity in *John 17*. Shortly before his arrest, betrayal, and death to take away the sins of the world, Jesus prayed for the unity and protection of present and future disciples. He asked our Father to glorify himself by bringing unity to his current and future disciples through Christ's atoning sacrifice.

Jesus prayed that his disciples would be "one," just as he and the Father are one. Jesus desired unity amongst his disciples so that the world would know the Father sent him and that he loves his disciples just as he loves Jesus. Jesus prayed that the reconciling and unifying love the Father has for his Son would be found in Jesus' followers *(John 17:11-26)*.

Jesus died and rose from the dead so that his followers would be reconciled to God, and would also experience and pursue this unifying, reconciling love for one another. The reconciliation and unity of disciples scattered throughout the earth is part of the gift of eternal life for which Jesus died, and testifies to the world of the power of the gospel. The reconciled community of Jesus' disciples is to be a community marked by love for God and for one another *(Mark 12:30-31)*, both now and into eternity.

QUESTIONS TO CONSIDER

- Do you see racial reconciliation as an important gospel issue? Is that a new concept for you?
- In what ways have you seen God bring unity in your relationships with Christians from different ethnic backgrounds?
- Is there anybody in your life you need to seek reconciliation with? Take some time to ask God to bring about reconciliation and lead you in seeking unity.
- Are there ways you and your spouse or another family member have different views regarding racial reconciliation? How can you look to the gospel together in this?

FURTHER READING

- By faith in Christ, we are reconciled to God: *Romans 5:6-11; 2 Corinthians 5:16-21; Ephesians 1:3-2:22*
- Ethnically diverse groups of people have equal access to God and the Spirit by faith in Christ: *Acts 2:1-40; Ephesians 2:11-3:13*
- Jesus' disciples are to be marked by love for God and one another: *Mark 12:30-31; John 13:35; Acts 13:1*

TALKING WITH KIDS

GOALS WHEN TEACHING YOUR CHILD

- Help your child to understand what reconciliation looks like, and how the gospel brings about reconciliation between different people and groups.

- Explain to your child why it is important to always forgive people and seek reconciliation, even when it's hard.

- Help your child to see that we are able to be reconciled to other people because God came to reconcile us first. Jesus came to heal us, forgive us, and bring us back into full friendship with our Creator and other people.

WORDS TO EXPLAIN TO YOUR CHILD

- **Reconciliation:** The restoration of a previously broken relationship between people.
- **Unity:** When people are peacefully joined together in love even when there is disagreement.

SCRIPTURE READING & REFLECTION WITH YOUR CHILD

Read the story of the Prodigal Son from *Luke 15:11-32*. Discuss how God is a loving Father who wants to welcome us home.

WAYS TO PRAY WITH YOUR CHILD

- Pray for people who believe the lie of racism, that the Holy Spirit would open their eyes to the truth that all people are made in God's image.

- Pray that God would bring all Christians together in unity as one family in Jesus, and that God would remove all forms of division from our hearts.

- Has anyone in your life made your child feel bad because they're different from them? Ask God to help your child to forgive them and seek reconciliation with them. Help your child understand how to respond wisely when this person is cruel.

- Does your child know anyone who seems very different from them? Ask God how you and your child can reach out to show the love and kindness of Jesus to them.

Conclusion

THE GOSPEL IN COLOR

Curtis A. Woods and Jarvis J. Williams

CELEBRATING THE GOSPEL'S GOODNESS

The gospel of Jesus Christ proclaims the best news possible, bringing with it the power to heal every painful rift and wound that the world has known. The sufficiency of Jesus' death for the many colorful sinners in the world is testified by the historical fact that God raised him up from the dead. Consequently, the gospel of the crucified, resurrected, and glorified Christ freely offers to every tongue, tribe, people, and nation God's solution for the problem of racism and ethnic division and his provision for reconciliation. Through the death and resurrection of Jesus, the one and true living God and Father of the Lord Jesus Christ becomes the God of Jews and Gentiles with many different colors of skin *(Romans 3:21-30)*.

SEEING THE STORY IN FULL COLOR

Imagine some friends invite you over to their house, and boast about how they have an incredible entertainment system. Sitting down, these friends show you their black-and-white television set, and ask if you are impressed with how modern it is. You would likely counsel your friends to get an upgrade, because they are not seeing the images on the TV as they were intended. A color screen gives a fuller picture, showing the image as it was meant to be seen.

That's what seeing the gospel in color is all about.

We want to see children grow up knowing this full-color gospel, that they would see every image-bearer through the biblical lens of love instead of a false cultural lens of racial superiority and inferiority. Our dream is that all Christian parents would raise their children to view different skin colors with appreciation, because the gospel has transformed their worldview and approach to life.

It's been our honor and pleasure to seek to share the complicated story of race and the power of gospel-centered racial reconciliation in a way that parents and children can understand. Of course, it is ultimately up to each parent to shepherd their children's hearts through each section. Our great hope is that you find this book, and its companion *The Gospel in Color — For Kids*, to be helpful resources to go back to again and again, and that they help children learn to view God's glorious creation and salvation story in its radiant technicolor glory — the way it was meant to be seen.

TEN EXHORTATIONS

We'd like to conclude with some exhortations for parents. These may feel challenging, but they are things we would prescribe for ourselves as well! And as we all look to our Lord and rely on the power of the Spirit, he can equip and empower us in all areas of life, including the area of racial reconciliation. Here are ten goals for all Christian parents:

1. **Admit** where we have fallen in our understanding of the gospel and race. We all need help in this area.
2. **Give** fellow Christians a chance to express their sorrow and disappointment about issues of race and racism in a non-threatening environment.
3. **Create** opportunities for our children to build friendships with people who have different skin colors and life experiences.

4. **Remind** our children that they are fearfully and wonderfully made in the image of God, and that no color is better or worse than another color.
5. **Encourage** our children that Jesus doesn't just save us, but calls us to grow in following him. We have been saved to become disciples of Christ who properly love one another until our blessed Lord returns.
6. **Learn**, **practice**, and **help** our kids understand the whole gospel.
7. **Spend time** thinking critically and teaching our kids about race, racism, and racial injustice.
8. **Help** our kids understand how the gospel intersects with racial and ethnic diversity.
9. **Teach** our kids how to value and honor the beautiful colors of their skin as created by God, without seeing other colors of skin as inferior in any way.
10. **Teach** our kids to desire and celebrate the unification of all things and all colors in Christ.

A FURTHER RESOURCE

Again, we realize these are challenging things to walk through with your children — which is sadly why some parents don't talk about them at all. But we all need to be intentional, leaning on the Spirit as we look for moments to walk our kids through these issues and seize teachable opportunities as they come up in the course of everyday life.

We hope you've found *The Gospel in Color* books to be helpful companions when walking through important conversations, and that they will prompt times of thought, prayer, and reflection with your child, equipping him or her to view the world through a robust gospel lens.

Thanks for going on this journey with us. May our good and gracious Lord draw his people ever closer, until the day we celebrate him together in the new creation.

Patrol is a team of storytellers and artists producing books which tell fiction and non-fiction stories inspired by the Bible.

Jesus used storytelling to help people understand spiritual truths about the kingdom of God and its relation to our lives. Following his lead, we use imaginative stories and visuals to communicate biblical truths to all people, including everyday Christians.

Start reading along today!

WeArePatrol.com
@WeArePatrol

PRESENTED TO

FROM

DATE

THE GOSPEL IN COLOR - FOR KIDS

Text copyright © 2018 by Curtis A. Woods and Jarvis J. Williams
Illustration copyright © 2018 by Rommel Ruiz

All rights reserved. No part of this publication may be reproduced, distributed, or transmitted in any form or by any means, including photocopying, recording, or other electronic or mechanical methods, without the prior written permission of the publisher, except in the case of brief quotations embodied in critical reviews and certain other noncommercial uses permitted by copyright law.

First Edition 2018
Printed in China

ISBN-10: 0-9990835-8-9
ISBN-13: 978-0-9990835-8-1
ISBN-10: 0-9990835-9-7 (eBook)
ISBN-13: 978-0-9990835-9-8 (eBook)
Library of Congress Control Number: 2018943144

A **Patrol** Original Book

THE GOSPEL IN COLOR

EDITORIAL

CONTENT DIRECTOR
Eleazar Ruiz

WRITERS
Curtis A. Woods
Jarvis J. Williams

EDITOR
Pip Craighead

CREATIVE

ART DIRECTOR & ILLUSTRATOR
Rommel Ruiz

HEAD OF DESIGN
Eleazar Ruiz

Patrol is a team of storytellers and artists producing books which tell fiction and non-fiction stories inspired by the Bible.

Jesus used storytelling to help people understand spiritual truths about the kingdom of God and its relation to our lives. Following his lead, we use imaginative stories and visuals to communicate biblical truths to all people, including everyday Christians.

Start reading along today!

WeArePatrol.com
@WeArePatrol

CONTENTS

06 **Parents' Guide**
How to Use This Book

08 **Kids' Guide**
How to Use This Book

10 **Introduction**
What's This Book For, Anyway?

16 **Chapter 1**
What Is Race?

30 **Chapter 2**
What Is Racism?

44 **Chapter 3**
What Is the Good News of Jesus Christ?

56 **Chapter 4**
What Is Reconciliation?

72 **Conclusion**
The Gospel in Color

77 **Answer Key**

PARENTS' GUIDE
HOW TO USE THIS BOOK

This book is specifically designed so that your child can dig deep into what the Bible says about race, racism, and reconciliation. These are complex topics, which is why each chapter's content is presented in a way that can engage children at different age levels. To facilitate times of reflection and response, every chapter ends with activities for further study, thought, and prayer.

FOR CHILDREN AGES SIX TO NINE

We recommend reading each chapter with your child, pausing to point out the **Words to Know** definitions and enjoy the illustrations. The imagery and stories throughout the book are there to help your child grasp theological and historical concepts, giving concrete ways to explain creation, the fall, sin, the gospel, redemption, racism, and reconciliation.

After reading and talking about each chapter with your child, go through the **Read & Respond** section, reading the suggested Bible passage and then asking your child the accompanying questions. You can find the answers at the back of the book, and can use these to help coach your child into fully understanding the concepts therein. We suggest reviewing these chapters multiple times, reinforcing the concepts with each reading.

Kids of all ages can **Memorize Scripture**; we encourage you to write down the memory passage from each chapter and place it somewhere you and your child will see it often. Test your child frequently to help them absorb the passage until they know it well. Lastly, the **Ways to Pray** section is designed to help you spend time praying with your child based on the topics of each chapter, utilizing suggested prayer points as well as whatever prayer is on your heart based on the reading.

FOR UPPER ELEMENTARY STUDENTS (AGES TEN AND UP)

This book is also written so that older children can read the book independently. We'd recommend giving your child a journal to use when going through the book. Encourage them to jot down their thoughts and reactions to each chapter, answer questions, write the memory Scripture, and journal their prayers.

After your child has gone through each chapter, start conversations with them about the topics that chapter covered. Ask if there were statements they found challenging or surprising, and seek to explain theological and historical concepts to them as needed. The activity sections are there to help draw connections between theological concepts and children's everyday lives, so we encourage you to ask questions based on those frameworks. Additionally, ask if your child can think of Bible stories and Scripture passages that connect with the themes of each chapter, and make connections to what your church is currently learning on Sundays. Prayer is a vital part of the process, so take time to pray with your child based on what they're learning and how these topics are touching their heart.

KIDS' GUIDE
HOW TO USE THIS BOOK

This book is designed so that kids — like you — can dig deep into what the Bible says about race, racism, and reconciliation. To help you better understand the topics we'll be exploring, each chapter ends with activities for you to complete. This book is also made so that a parent can go through their own version of the book, *The Gospel in Color — For Parents*. Each chapter in that book covers the same themes and highlights the same vocab words, so that you can talk with your parent, ask questions, and pray as you learn together.

Below are the activity sections to keep an eye out for:
- **Read & Respond**: Answer questions based on the Scripture reading for each chapter.
- **Memorize Scripture**: Write down a Scripture relevant to the chapter's theme and commit it to memory.

- **Ways to Pray**: Spend time praying based on the topics of each chapter, utilizing suggested prayer points as well as whatever prayer is on your heart based on the reading.

Our hope is not only that you have fun completing these activities, but that above all, you connect with Jesus through them. God tells us that he is always with us, and so we can talk to him at any point, whether we have questions or simply want to thank him for his goodness. He loves us and promises to hear us when we're seeking him. And that is a wonderful truth indeed.

INTRODUCTION

WHAT'S THIS BOOK FOR, ANYWAY?

BY CURTIS A. WOODS
& JARVIS J. WILLIAMS

BIG IDEA

Racism is real, and it is a sin. All sin is ultimately a spiritual problem, which means it can only find complete healing through Jesus. This book will help you have honest conversations about race, ethnic differences, and racial reconciliation — because Jesus came to heal all our brokenness, including that of racism.

H ave you ever wondered why groups of people look different from one another? Beyond just the differences in the ways people dress or do their hairstyles, people from all over the world look different. Just like a box of crayons, human beings come in a wide variety of colors. But no matter what color our skin is, it's not an accident. It's actually part of God's good design.

As we'll learn together in this book, the Bible tells us that God made human beings "in his image" — meaning they reflect the nature of God. That's something that's true of all people, no matter where they come from or what they look like. God doesn't want us all to look and act exactly the same. The fact that we are all different is actually very beautiful, particularly when we come together to worship Jesus as one big family, just as we see in the book of *Revelation* at the very end of the Bible.

Just like a talent show, all groups of people and all cultures have something special to share with the world. God made us so that in our differences, we would all be unified in our love for Christ.

THE UGLY IDEA

But an idea you have probably heard of — racism — tries to turn God's design upside down. Instead of agreeing with the Bible that all people are made in God's image and are equally valuable, racism says that some people are more valuable than others. This is a complete lie. And like all lies, it causes great pain.

People who believe the lie of racism can do terrible things, whether they're saying something cruel about someone who is different from them or actually attacking them physically. People have killed other people for racist reasons, yet sometimes racism is far more subtle and sneaky — so sneaky it seems almost invisible at first. Racism can be present in words and actions that seem polite, but are actually subtle ways of letting people know they're less valuable because they're different.

In this book, we'll learn about where the lie of racism comes from — and how Jesus wants us to fight this lie.

**RACISM SAYS THAT SOME PEOPLE ARE MORE VALUABLE THAN OTHERS. THIS IS A COMPLETE LIE.
AND LIKE ALL LIES, IT CAUSES GREAT PAIN.**

PRETENDING NOT TO SEE

Have you ever heard the word *color-blind*? Being color-blind is a medical condition some people have in which they can't see certain colors. But color-blind is a term with two meanings. Besides describing a medical condition, it can also be used to describe an idea about race some people have. They think that to fight the evil of racism, we should all just pretend not to see the fact that people have different skin colors. They say that we shouldn't acknowledge the fact that we're different, and should just treat everyone the same.

WORD TO KNOW

COLOR-BLINDNESS
The idea that we should ignore people's ethnic differences.

While it's definitely good to treat all people with kindness and respect, that doesn't mean we should pretend that everyone's skin colors are all the same. People around the world have all sorts of different skin colors — and that's not a bad thing. In fact, it's part of God's design!

Instead of pretending that people don't have different skin colors or that racism doesn't exist, we need to discuss these things. **Color-blindness** won't make racism go away, which is why we need to talk about where racism comes from and how it hurts people. And that's why this book exists.

WHAT THIS BOOK IS ALL ABOUT

This book was written to help you understand different skin colors, ethnic differences, and the evil of racism from a Christian perspective.

The Bible not only shows us where racism ultimately comes from, it tells us how to fight it, and it shows us why all people have dignity and value. Jesus gives us the power to end racism, and the Bible shows us how Jesus' followers accepted and loved each other, no matter how differently they looked or acted.

Each chapter in this book discusses important concepts, and features vivid illustrations to help show the ideas we're talking about. The end of every chapter contains activities, as well as ways to pray so that after reading, you can spend some time talking to Jesus about what you're learning. This book is also designed so that you can learn along with a parent or friend, so that both of you can grow in understanding the Bible and one another.

We're excited to go on this journey with you, and hope you are too! God's word — the Bible — is filled with truth that can change the world and bring healing to our hearts, and Jesus wants to help us understand the power of his love and how it applies to issues of race.

CHAPTER 1
WHAT IS RACE?
BY CURTIS A. WOODS

BIG IDEA

The beginning of the Bible tells us how God made the world. God created everything good, and all people were made in his image, which means that all people have equal value and worth. Yet some people believe a lie about race that says that some types of people are better than others. Instead of believing this lie, God wants us to honor every skin color.

BEGINNINGS ARE IMPORTANT

Have you ever watched part of a movie, but missed the beginning? Often it can be a confusing experience, as you try to figure out who is who and where the story is going. That's why beginnings are so important — they help us understand what is happening and what to expect in the future.

In our lives today, many people are deeply confused because, just like someone missing the start of a movie, they don't know the beginning of the story of the world. That's one of the reasons God graciously gave us the Bible, which tells us all we need to know about how things began. So when we have questions about skin color, racism, and human relationships, we first look to the Bible, because the Bible shows us the true story of the world. Having a biblical view is key.

WHAT IS RACE?

THE BEGINNING OF ALL BEGINNINGS

The Bible is made up of different books, and the very first book is called *Genesis* — which literally means "beginning." The beginning of *Genesis* tells us how God created the world out of nothing by speaking light into existence. He made the heavens and the earth. On the earth, he gathered the waters together into the sea and made the dry land appear. God decorated the earth with vegetation that could reproduce all kinds of seeds, fruit, and trees. God made all these things good.

God made the sun and moon, and then he made the land animals and sea creatures — living things which were different but all wonderful. All these creatures were fruitful and multiplied their species on the earth and in the sea. God was pleased with what he had made.

Lastly, God created his crowning jewel — Adam and Eve — in his image, placing them in the Garden of Eden. God made this man and woman so that they would reproduce other stewards over his creation and carry out God's creation mandate together. No other creature could help them fulfill God's command. God was so excited about his creation that he rested to enjoy his artistry.

The story of creation presents a beautiful picture of love. God cared for his creation by crafting a world that could sustain the physical and emotional needs of humanity. The man and woman loved and trusted one another without fear. The animals and sea creatures enjoyed their habitats without territorial fighting. It was literally *all good*!

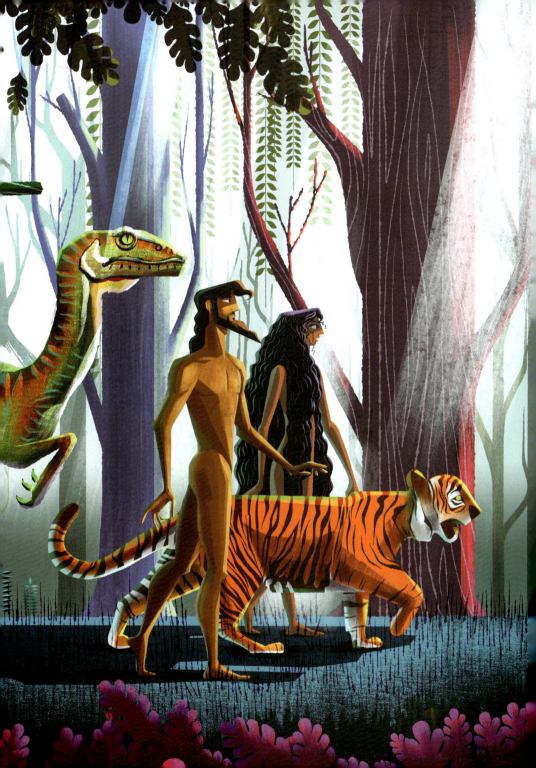

THE TRUTH ABOUT RACE

The Bible clearly tells us that God created every family from the loving relationship of the first family, Adam and Eve. According to Scripture, every human comes from this same family *(Acts 17:26)*. Every person on earth is made in God's image, and as such, has a unique worth and identity. And all people are **equal** because they are all made in the image of God.

> **WORD TO KNOW**
>
> **EQUAL**
> Having the same worth and value.

Every skin color on the earth points back to the first person created from the earth — Adam. Therefore, God's vision is for all colors to love one another truly, as equals. The Bible rejects the idea of a special race of people who sit above other skin colors.

THE LIE ABOUT RACE

But over time, some people began believing a lie about people who looked different than they did. They said that there are different types of humans, and that some humans are better than others. This imaginary concept of **race** was developed to separate humans based on color. Unlike God's intention to have beautiful variety within his creation, this idea of race lifts up one skin color on the backs of other colors. These racial categories make some people feel better than others, giving them a sense of superiority.

As an example, many Europeans in the 18th century believed they were special above all other cultures. False teachers of the time taught others to see people with dark or brown skin color as inferior beings — despite the fact that they all had the same color of blood running through their veins.

Not only is this very sad, it goes against what God intended. The Bible shows us that there is ultimately only one race: the human race. True love for other colors will never label different hues inferior, and relationships suffer when some people think they are better than other people.

> **WORD TO KNOW**
>
> **RACE**
> A word which can simply refer to the human race or a specific ethnic group, but which can be falsely used to mean a category of people with an inherently different value than other people.

EVERY COLOR WAS MADE TO BE LOVED AND CHERISHED,
BECAUSE GOD CREATED ALL THINGS GOOD.

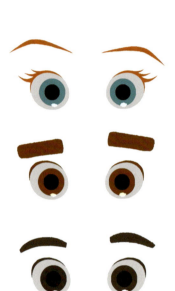

NEW EYES

God wants to give us new eyes to see all the colors of humanity without fear or anger. Every color was made to be loved and cherished, because God created all things good.

You are a part of God's original good creation. He created you the way you are. All human colors are special since they bear God's image.

So where does the destructive lie of racism actually come from? What is its ultimate root? The beginning of the Bible contains the answer to those questions, as we'll see in the next chapter!

READ & RESPOND

Read the creation account in *Genesis 1-2* and answer the following questions.

1. In *Genesis 1:31*, what did God say when he surveyed everything that he had made?

2. What does *Genesis 1:26-27* tell us about all human beings? In whose image are they made?

3. What does this tell us about the value of people of different skin colors?

4. How do you think God wants you to treat other people made in the image of God through your thoughts, speech, and actions regardless of whether those people share your skin color?

MEMORIZE SCRIPTURE

Write down the following Scripture and commit it to memory: *Psalm 139:14.*

WAYS TO PRAY

Below are prayer points to help you talk to God about what you're learning. We encourage you to speak to him in your own words, knowing he is always ready to hear his children.

- Give God thanks for the fact that he made the world and all things in it, and praise him that you have the honor of being made in the image of God.

- Give God praise that the way he made you — including your skin color and ethnic background — is no mistake, and that your skin color and ethnic heritage are good.

Pray that God would give you eyes to see his hand in the wonderful diversity of all people in the world, and thank him that he is the God of every tribe, tongue, people, and nation.

Write your own prayer to God, in your own words, based on the topics covered in this chapter.

CHAPTER 2

WHAT IS RACISM?

BY CURTIS A. WOODS

BIG IDEA

The Bible tells us that God created our world good, but when people rebelled against God, sin appeared. Sin brought evil and sadness into our world, and is the reason people hurt and hate one another. The lie of racism has led to great pain and evil, and still hurts people today. That's why it's so important that we look to Jesus and speak truth.

THE BIG LIE

As we saw in the last chapter, God made the world very good. Adam and Eve dwelled in a beautiful garden, living in harmony with God and each other. But one day, something terrible happened — something which led to all the other sad things in the world today, including racism.

Genesis 3 tells us a serpent lied to Eve, saying that God wanted to withhold something good from the first family. Eve listened to the serpent and the desires of her own heart, questioning God's goodness.

WORD TO KNOW

SIN
An act of rebellion against God and his good laws.

Eve doubted God's word, and decided to do things her way instead of God's. She wanted to act like her own god by obeying her own sinful desires.

Both Adam and Eve chose to believe the big lie: that God could not be trusted.

When Adam and Eve believed this lie and disobeyed God, **sin** entered humanity. Sin is rebellion against God and his commands, and it is the cause of everything sad and wrong in our world.

> **WORD TO KNOW**
>
> **RACISM**
> The poisonous idea of people or governments rewarding social and economic privileges to one group of people by virtue of skin color or ethnic background.

Adam and Eve's sin led to global strife on earth. Men and women had fights with one another. The process of farming and getting food became burdensome. Animals attacked humans and ate other animals. God had created a peaceful, beautiful world, but sin birthed chaos. The chaos of sin means that creation experiences disorder, trouble, and confusion.

THE SIN OF RACISM

Because of sin, our world is filled with struggle, and the serpent continues to spread lies about God's original good creation. Over the many centuries since Adam and Eve, people have been deceived by these lies and have shared them with other people. One of these lies is **racism**, which is based on the false concept of race that we talked about in the last chapter.

The lie of racism was widespread through Europe during the 18th century and beyond. Instead of believing that all humans were ultimately one race created by God, people taught the lie that God created multiple races of humans. Many of these thinkers viewed some people as members of different species. In other words, they said that people who were different than them were not fully human. This is a lie from the old serpent, and goes against what the Bible teaches.

Some people even tried to distort what the Bible says to support their racist beliefs. Imagine how God feels when people twist his word to support lies. That's why it is so important to read the Bible the way the Author meant it to be understood, and to avoid reading racist ideas into biblical stories.

RACISM AND SLAVERY

One of the saddest things about the history of racism is how people who had the power to bully others treated certain image-bearers like disposable items. They labeled some colors superior and others inferior. In world history, "lesser" colors were captured, placed in warehouses, and transported all over the globe like cargo in the bottom of rat-filled boats. Children were kidnapped from their mothers and fathers. Whole families were put in chains, then separated and sold — they were

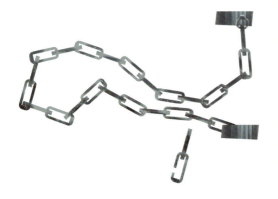

treated just like property. People often died during these voyages to slave ports around the world.

This was something that many Europeans and Americans did to Africans over the centuries, before it was made illegal. Like true bullies, the villains who kidnapped, bought, and sold these victims did not believe enslaved people possessed human dignity. The truth is that anytime we treat humans like disposable items it delights the devil, but dishonors God.

RACISM CAUSES GREAT PAIN

Racism — even when it doesn't involve slavery — is still around today. Racism often happens when a society passes laws that make it hard for certain people to succeed. Racism takes place when certain skin colors are labeled problems even before problems occur. Racism can happen in sneaky ways as well as obvious ones. Racism occurs when people don't get a job just because they have a certain skin color or look different.

ALL CHRISTIANS ARE CALLED TO HONOR GOD BY SPEAKING THE TRUTH AGAINST RACISM IN A GRACIOUS WAY.

Have you ever played a game like "cooties," where you pretend that somebody has an imaginary disease, and that you can't touch them? The game can become mean, as children laugh and point at some innocent child falsely declared "cooties." That child can end up feeling shamed, hurt, and alone.

That's what racism does in society. It hurts and shames people who have been labeled "problems." Racism is profoundly evil.

WHERE DO WE GO FROM HERE?

All Christians are called to honor God by speaking the truth against racism in a gracious way. That means you no longer see people who have racist ideas as the enemy. They are victims of your enemy. When you encounter a person who hates people because of their skin color, you are hearing the serpent's voice.

But there's good news — incredibly good news, as a matter of fact. Racism will not be victorious in our world, because Jesus came to heal the impact that Adam and Eve's sin brought upon the entire world. In the next chapter, we'll talk about how Jesus restores our relationship with God and each other, and brings victory over racism and every other sin.

READ & RESPOND

Read the account of the fall of humanity in Genesis 3 and answer the following questions.

1. According to Genesis 3:1-6, how does sin start? What kind of attitude did Adam and Eve have toward God?

2. What were the consequences of Adam and Eve's sin?

3. How does the sin of racism directly go against what God says in the Bible?

4. How does racism hurt people today?

MEMORIZE SCRIPTURE

Write down the following Scripture and commit it to memory: *Romans 6:23.*

WAYS TO PRAY

Below are prayer points to help you talk to God about what you're learning. We encourage you to speak to him in your own words, knowing he is always ready to hear his children.

> Pray that Jesus would help you see all people as worthy of dignity and respect because they are made in the image of God.

Have you ever been cruel to someone because they were different, whether they had a different skin color or simply acted differently than you? If so, ask God for forgiveness for that sin, and ask him to give you wisdom in how to apologize to that person, if at all possible.

Is there anybody you have a hard time showing kindness to because they are different than you? Ask the Lord to help you see that person the way he would have you see them — as someone loved by God.

Is there anybody in your life who you have heard say something racist? If so, pray for that person, and ask God for wisdom on any ways you can lovingly, graciously correct those words (check in with your parent for advice on this). Ask God to heal any pain those racist words have caused you.

> **Write your own prayer to God, in your own words, based on the topics covered in this chapter.**

CHAPTER 3

WHAT IS THE GOOD NEWS OF JESUS CHRIST?

BY JARVIS J. WILLIAMS

BIG IDEA

The gospel is the good news that Jesus came to undo the curse of sin that came as a result of Adam and Eve's rebellion. Instead of giving up on his people, God sent his Son to live a perfect life, die on the cross, and rise again, forgiving us of our sins — including the sin of racism. Jesus brings healing to all the world's divisions.

VERY, VERY, VERY GOOD NEWS

You know the feeling of sharing good news with a friend? Maybe the good news is that you made a new friend, or that someone you know who was sick is now feeling better. Whatever the news, it is exciting to share something happy with someone else.

Well, the Bible contains something very special: it contains the best news that anyone has ever heard! In fact, you could call it very, very, very good news — the best news of all. But to really understand this good news, we have to look at the whole story of the Bible.

Ready? Let's go!

THE PROBLEM OF SIN

As we saw in Chapter 1, the Bible starts with God making the whole world — the planets, sun, and stars, as well as our earth and everything in it. He made the animals and then, last of all, he made the first people, Adam and Eve. Adam and Eve lived in a beautiful garden, and were friends with God. Being friends with God is a wonderful thing — it's actually the most wonderful thing there is.

But after Adam and Eve believed the lie and disobeyed God, their relationship with God and with each other was broken. When they rebelled against God, sin came into the world — and when sin came, it ruined everything.

Because of sin, people aren't friends with God anymore.

Because of sin, people and the rest of creation experience death.

Because of sin, people fight with each other and say hurtful things to one another.

Because of sin, people don't like each other because of how they look or what color their skin is.

Sin is the reason there is so much sadness in the world, and it is the big problem beneath every other problem. Every war, every death, every sad thing is because of sin.

GOD LOVES PEOPLE TOO MUCH TO LET THE STORY END WITH ADAM AND EVE'S SIN.

HOPE FOR THE WORLD

God loves people too much to let the story end with Adam and Eve's sin. In fact, he promised his people that one day, there would come a Savior to rescue the world from sin and death.

Many centuries passed, and during that time, sin led to more and more trouble, pain, and evil. One of those evils is called *division*, which is what happens when people refuse to be friends with people who are somehow different than them. Racism, which we talked about in the previous chapter, is a form of sinful division.

But about 2,000 years ago, to everyone's surprise, God himself came into the story of our world to rescue it! Jesus Christ was born a Jewish man, but while he was fully a human being, he was also God. It's hard to completely understand how such a thing could be, but nothing is impossible for God.

HOW JESUS BRINGS HEALING

Jesus lived a perfect life, healing people, showing love to people, and sharing the news of God's kingdom. Jesus invited people into God's kingdom, telling them that God cared about them and wanted them to act in love and kindness with one another the way that Jesus acted in love and kindness.

Jesus showed his love in the most powerful way possible: by dying for our sins. See, each of us has sinned in our lives one way or another, and since sin is an act of rebellion against God, it deserves punishment. In addition to our personal sins, the presence of sin has messed up the whole world. But since God wants to forgive us, he actually took the punishment for our sin himself when Jesus died upon the cross.

After Jesus died, he was buried in a rock tomb. But three days later, he rose again — he was no longer dead, but alive forevermore. The **resurrection** of Jesus shows that God is stronger than death. After his resurrection, Jesus told his followers to go and tell the whole world about him.

> **WORD TO KNOW**
>
> **RESURRECTION**
>
> The act of someone being raised from death to life. Jesus was resurrected after his death on the cross, and because of Jesus, all who believe in his name have the future promise of being raised from death to everlasting life.

> **WORD TO KNOW**
>
> **GOSPEL**
> The good news that through Jesus' life, death, resurrection, and ascension (going into heaven to rule our world with his Father), the kingdom of God has come and all can be saved through faith in him.

Because Jesus is alive, the whole world can experience forgiveness and healing.

Because Jesus is alive, death will ultimately be done away with.

Because Jesus is alive, people can be friends with God forever!

That's the very, very, very good news we talked about at the beginning of this chapter. The **gospel** is the good news of Jesus' life, death, and resurrection, which brings the kingdom of God to our world. The gospel results in the forgiveness of sin — including the sin of racism. That means that followers of Jesus should no longer be divided because of how they look or what color their skin is.

This is good news for our world! In the next chapter, we'll talk about how the gospel powerfully brings about reconciliation to people divided by racism.

READ & RESPOND

Read 1 Corinthians 15:20-23 and answer the following questions.

1 Who is the man who brought death in 1 Corinthians 15:21, and who is the man who brought the resurrection of the dead?

2 How does Jesus' death pay the price for all our sins? What does that mean for your life and your sins?

3 How is Jesus' life, death, and resurrection the greatest reason for rejoicing that we could ever hear? How does it bring healing to the world, including people of every skin color?

4 What do you think it means to "belong to Christ" as mentioned in 1 Corinthians 15:23? How can you live as somebody who belongs to Christ, including through the way you treat people of different skin colors and backgrounds?

MEMORIZE SCRIPTURE

Write down the following Scripture and commit it to memory: *John 1:29*.

WAYS TO PRAY

Below are prayer points to help you talk to God about what you're learning. We encourage you to speak to him in your own words, knowing he is always ready to hear his children.

> Thank God for the forgiveness and redemption we have in Jesus' freely given sacrifice. Rejoice in the fact that the Lord counts you as a beloved son or daughter because you've put your faith in him.

Pray that everyone in your family would continually turn to Jesus for forgiveness and restoration whenever they sin, knowing that Christ has already paid the price for sinners — including if they sin by regarding one skin color as better than another.

Pray that people all over the world who do not know Jesus would come to experience forgiveness and peace with God through the gospel. Pray that this good news would bring healing to all those who are divided over skin color and other issues.

Is there anyone you know who you'd like to share the good news of Jesus with? Ask God how you can tell them about Jesus, and pray for an opportunity to share this exciting news with them. Ask your parent for advice on how to share the gospel.

Write your own prayer to God, in your own words, based on the topics covered in this chapter.

CHAPTER 4
WHAT IS RECONCILIATION

BY JARVIS J. WILLIAMS

BIG IDEA

Jesus came to bring peace between all sorts of people — no matter how different they may seem. This reconciliation is one of the results of the gospel, and brings healing to the divisions caused by racism. In Jesus, God calls his people to love and forgive one another, regardless of our countries, cultures, or colors.

THE SON WHO RAN AWAY

Have you ever been cruel to someone, or had someone be cruel to you? It can cause great pain and sadness to everyone involved. But when someone says sorry, that is the start of **reconciliation** – when two people who were separated as enemies come together as friends.

During his ministry on earth, Jesus told his followers a powerful story about reconciliation. It's known as the story of the Prodigal Son.

GOD IS A LOVING FATHER WHO WANTS TO WELCOME US HOME.

> **WORD TO KNOW**
>
> **RECONCILIATION**
> The restoration of a previously broken relationship between people.

A father had two sons. The older son worked hard for his father, but one day, the younger son asked his father to give him money so that he could do what he wanted with it. The father gave his son what he asked for. The younger son left his family to go away to a far country, where he wasted all of his money on partying and selfish things.

After wasting his money, the younger son was hungry, so hungry that he even wished he could eat what pigs eat. So he went back home to beg for his father's forgiveness and ask if he could work hard for his father in exchange for food. Do you think the father would be happy to see his younger son, or angry with how selfishly his son had left the family and wasted all his money?

Well, when the father saw his younger son coming from a distance, he rushed to meet him. He embraced him and kissed him. He was so thankful to have his son home.

The father celebrated his son's return with a party. The older son who had stayed home and served his father complained that his father had showed his younger son too much affection. The father told his older son that the son who returned was lost, but now was found. His return home was a reason to celebrate!

WHAT IS RECONCILIATION?

GOD RECONCILES US

The father's response to his younger son is a beautiful picture of reconciliation. The younger son acted as an enemy when he abandoned his father. But when he returned to his father after coming to his senses, the father received his son as a friend. This is what reconciliation is all about.

Reconciliation is something we all need. That's actually what the good news of Jesus is all about — God came to reconcile us even though we had sinned against him and treated him as an enemy. Jesus came to heal us, forgive us, and bring us back into full friendship with our Creator and other people. Jesus came to reconcile the entire world, the entire universe, to himself!

God is a loving Father who wants to welcome us home.

GOD BRINGS US TOGETHER

Reconciliation is not only something that happens between us and God. It's also something that God brings about between ourselves and other people — including people divided over race. Reconciliation is not optional!

As we've seen in previous chapters, the sin of racism makes people enemies of one another based on their skin colors or where they come from. But Jesus came to reconcile enemies and make them friends. Jesus died on the cross for all our sins — including the sin of racism. As a result, people who believe in Jesus are brothers and sisters in Christ, no matter what we look like.

In fact, Jesus brings together all sorts of different people — from every tribe and people and language all over the world — and makes them one big family: the family of God. Because they are God's family, all followers of Jesus are to peacefully live with one another despite their differences — in **unity**. For Christians, we must absolutely oppose racism, because it is an attack upon our unity as brothers and sisters in Christ.

> **WORD TO KNOW**
>
> **UNITY**
> When people are peacefully joined together in love even when there is disagreement.

FORGIVING THOSE WHO SIN AGAINST US

Jesus calls us to love our neighbor as ourselves — which means we should treat people in a way that shows them they are loved and valued, because Jesus loves and values them. Loving people also means forgiving them if they do something wrong to us, including if they display racism by their words or actions. Forgiveness can feel very hard sometimes. Jesus knows how hard it can be — he died on the cross in order to forgive us, even though it was the most painful experience possible. But because Jesus died on the cross, he enables us to forgive people for their sins against us.

Forgiving someone doesn't mean we pretend we aren't hurt, and it doesn't mean we just ignore whatever they do. Forgiveness means we don't retaliate with hate, but commit to loving them instead. Even when we forgive someone, the process of reconciliation means they

must still seek to make things right, undo damage they've done, and face the consequences of their actions.

We can't do these things on our own — so we must ask Jesus to help us to do them. We can rely on his power and help to forgive others, to seek reconciliation, and to display unity as followers of Jesus. In so doing, we help show people how great and wonderful God is, and that he is stronger than any evil, including racism!

READ & RESPOND

Read the story of the Prodigal Son from *Luke 15:11-32* and answer the following questions.

1 In *Luke 15:20-24*, how do we see the father in the story seek reconciliation with his son?

2 In *Luke 15:18-21*, what attitude did the son have when seeking reconciliation with his father?

3 What would it look like if the father and son had not reconciled?

4 Why might some people not want to seek reconciliation with people who are different from them?

MEMORIZE SCRIPTURE

Write down the following Scripture and commit it to memory: *Romans 5:10*.

WAYS TO PRAY

Below are prayer points to help you talk to God about what you're learning. We encourage you to speak to him in your own words, knowing he is always ready to hear his children.

> Pray for people who believe the lie of racism, that the Holy Spirit would open their eyes to the truth that all people are made in God's image.

Pray that God would bring all Christians together in unity as one family in Jesus, and that God would change us and remove all forms of racism from our hearts.

Has anyone in your life made you feel bad because you're different from them? Ask God to help you to forgive them and seek reconciliation with them. Ask your mom or dad for advice on how to respond when this person is cruel.

Is there anyone you know who seems very different from you? Ask God how you can reach out to show the love and kindness of Jesus to them.

Write your own prayer to God, in your own words, based on the topics covered in this chapter.

CONCLUSION
THE GOSPEL IN COLOR

**BY CURTIS A. WOODS
& JARVIS J. WILLIAMS**

SEEING THE STORY IN FULL COLOR

Imagine if some friends told you they have an incredible TV, and invite you over to their house to see it. But when they show you their TV, it only displays black and white pictures, with no color. Your friends would be missing out on a dazzling variety of colors, and not seeing movies and shows as they were made to be seen. A color screen gives a fuller picture, showing the image as it was intended to be.

That's why it's so important that we see God's world as it was meant to be seen — in color! And that's why this book is called *The Gospel in Color*, because we want everyone to see the good news of Jesus in all its glorious fullness and color.

Our hope is that kids, parents, and teachers alike would celebrate the fact that Jesus came to set us free from the sin of racism, and to bring racial reconciliation to all people. This is good news, and the whole world needs to hear it!

FIVE WAYS TO LIVE OUT THE GOSPEL IN COLOR

The gospel isn't something we're supposed to just learn about — it's something that's supposed to affect how we live our daily lives. To help you in that process, below are five ways you can live out the gospel in color. These may not always be easy to do, but if we look to Jesus and rely on the power of his Spirit, he will guide and equip us as we seek to follow him together.

1. **Become** friends with people who are different than you — whether they come from a different country, have a different skin color, or speak a different language. Just because someone is different doesn't mean you can't be wonderful friends, especially if you are both followers of Jesus.
2. **Admit** when you may see people with different skin colors as enemies. Instead of being fearful or mean to them, seek to pursue friendship and reconciliation with them.
3. Always **remember** that you are wonderfully made in the image of God, and that no color is better or worse than another color.

4. **Be honest** when you feel sad, angry, or hurt because of racism. Share your feelings with a parent or trusted friend, and most importantly, talk to God about how this makes you feel. Listen to other people when they express how they are affected by racism as well.

5. **Share** the gospel in color with other people! Tell them how Jesus came to set us free from sin and heal all divisions, including those based on skin color. This good news is something to celebrate every day and tell other people about. Jesus told us to proclaim the gospel to the whole world — which means people of every skin color, language, and nation!

A FINAL ENCOURAGEMENT

We hope you've found this book to be a helpful companion for understanding race, reconciliation, and the life-changing power of the gospel. Our prayer is that you've experienced wonderful times of discussion and prayer when reading this with a parent or friend.

We're honored to have been able to share this book with you, and we thank you for going on this journey with us. Together, let's keep looking to Jesus and continue to pray that he will draw his people closer together, until the day we all celebrate him in the new creation!

ANSWER KEY

CHAPTER 1
WHAT IS RACE?

1. **In *Genesis 1:31*, what did God say when he surveyed everything that he had made?**
   God said that it was very good.

2. **What does *Genesis 1:26-27* tell us about all human beings? In whose image are they made?**
   All people, male and female, are made in the image of God, and have been given dominion over their fellow creatures.

3. **What does this tell us about the value of people of different skin colors?**
   That we are all equally made in the image of God.

4. **How do you think God wants you to treat other people made in the image of God through your thoughts, speech, and actions — regardless of whether those people share your skin color?**
   God wants us to treat all people with dignity, respect, and love in what we think, say, and do.

CHAPTER 2
WHAT IS RACISM?

1. **According to *Genesis 3:1-6*, how does sin start? What kind of attitude did Adam and Eve have toward God?**

   Adam and Eve listened to the serpent rather than God. Instead of trusting the Lord, they doubted that what God said was true and that his way was what was best for them.

2. **What were the consequences of Adam and Eve's sin?**

   Death. Their eyes were opened, they became aware of their nakedness, and they hid from God's presence. They sought to blame others for their choices, and from that point on, experienced pain and struggle in their lives. They were cast out from Eden and would eventually die, returning to the ground from which they were taken.

3. **How does the sin of racism directly go against what God says in the Bible?**

   Racism denies that all people are made in the image of God and shows the kind of partiality that God forbids. Instead of loving our neighbor as ourselves, racism shows love to some and cruelty to others.

4. **How does racism hurt people today?**

   Racism excludes people on an individual and group level.

CHAPTER 3
WHAT IS THE GOOD NEWS OF JESUS CHRIST?

1. **Who is the man who brought death in *1 Corinthians 15:21*, and who is the man who brought the resurrection of the dead?**
   Adam is the man who brought death; Jesus is the man who brought resurrection from the dead.

2. **How does Jesus' death pay the price for all our sins? What does that mean for your life and your sins?**
   Jesus' perfect life fulfilled the law, and he died in our place on the cross, taking our sin upon himself in order to bring about reconciliation between us and God. This atoning death means that when you place your faith in Jesus, you are forgiven and have peace with God.

3. **How is Jesus' life, death, and resurrection the greatest reason for rejoicing that we could ever hear? How does it bring healing to the world, including people of every skin color?**
   Jesus' life, death, and resurrection confront the problem for everything wrong and broken in our world: sin. Jesus came so that everybody everywhere could experience forgiveness for sin and restored fellowship with God and one another, regardless of their skin color and background.

4. **What do you think it means to "belong to Christ" as mentioned in *1 Corinthians 15:23*? How can you live as somebody who belongs to Christ, including through the way you treat people of different skin colors and backgrounds?**

   Answers may vary, but to belong to Christ is to be someone who has placed their faith in Jesus and is committed to following him. As a result, we will show gospel-motivated love to people of all skin colors and backgrounds, seeking to demonstrate and share the good news of Jesus with them.

CHAPTER 4
WHAT IS RECONCILIATION?

1. **In *Luke 15:20-24*, how do we see the father in the story seek reconciliation with his son?**

   He runs to his son and welcomes him back with open arms. The father clothes his son, shows him forgiveness, and throws a party to celebrate his son's return.

2. **In *Luke 15:18-21*, what attitude did the son have when seeking reconciliation with his father?**

   The son acknowledged his sin, said he was no longer worthy of his father's love, and hoped that his father would treat him as a hired servant instead of a son.

3. **What would it look like if the father and son had not reconciled?**

   Children can use their imaginations here, but in any case, the younger son would experience alienation and loneliness, while the father would not experience the joy of reunion with his son. Neither would experience reconciliation.

4. **Why might some people not want to seek reconciliation with people who are different from them?**
   A variety of answers are possible, including fear, hatred, unforgiveness, not understanding the gospel, not wishing to experience fellowship and unity with others who are different from them, etc.

NOTES

NOTES

NOTES